S0-BRY-850

CHANGE OF TERRITORY

The publication of this volume is supported in part by a grant from the Kentucky Arts Council with funds from the National Endowment for the Arts.

CHANGE OF TERRITORY

Poems by

Melvin Dixon

Volume One
in the Callaloo Poetry Series
Published at the University of Kentucky,
Lexington, 1983

Copyright © 1983 by Melvin Dixon.

Second Printing Melvin Dixon

All rights reserved under International and Pan-American Copyright Conventions.

A number of poems in this volume originally appeared in slightly different form in the following periodicals and are reprinted by permission: *The Beloit Poetry Journal, The Iowa Review, Parnassus, Callaloo, Freedomways, Présence Africaine, Okike, The Broadside Series, Obsidian, Black American Literature Forum, The Black Scholar,* and *Caliban.*

"Richard, Richard: *American Fuel*" and "Tour Guide: *La Maison des Esclaves*" were reprinted in the anthology, *Leaving the Bough: 50 American Poets of the 80s,* edited by Roger Gaess. Copyright 1982 by Roger Gaess. "Bobo Baoulé" was reprinted in *Southern Exposure.*

Lines 7-10 in "Richard, Richard: *American Fuel*" are taken from Richard Wright's unpublished diary. Quoted by permission of Mrs. Ellen Wright. Citations in "Fingering the Jagged Grains" are taken from *Romare Bearden: Collages: Profile/Part I: The Twenties.* Copyright 1978 by Cordier & Ekstrom. Used by permission of the publisher. "The Art of Romare Bearden" by Ralph Ellison. Copyright 1968 by Ralph Ellison. Used by permission of the author. *The Hero and the Blues* by Albert Murray. Copyright 1973 by Albert Murray. Used by permission of the author.

My thanks to the Massachusetts Arts and Humanities Foundation for a fellowship to complete some of the poems in this volume.

ISBN: 0-912759-04-6

Callaloo Poetry Series
University of Kentucky
Lexington, Kentucky 40506-0027

for my parents,
for Didier
and for
Richard,
navigators, all.

I like the sensation of being a total stranger in a strange place and sampling the strangeness of it until I find myself a little and get acquainted.

—Claude McKay

* * *

I was leaving the South to fling myself into the unknown, to meet other situations that would perhaps elicit from me other responses. And if I could meet enough of a different life, then, perhaps, gradually and slowly I might learn who I was, what I might be.

—Richard Wright

CONTENTS

I

CLIMBING MONTMARTRE

HUNGRY TRAVEL

I

Carolina mountains to Pee Dee town,
sharecropping, my father as a boy
led mules and siblings.
He plowed for fifty cents a week
until the day his house burned down.

"Everything lost in the flames,"
he tells my mother. "I don't know
how to give any more."
He takes her like the mule,
riding shotgun
back to Carolina cinders.

II

She croons, "Beautiful dreamer
wake unto me," as his arms lock
to her hips. He calls her, "Freak,
you must be some kind of freak."
She reaches for him, holds nothing.

In my twenty-fifth year,
his eyes avoiding mine, his voice:
"You're still my son," as if the silent
years between us were reasons to forget.
But I remember the song. I know
by heart her broken breath sung solo.

III

This poem for the three of us
pulling from one chain.

Our metallic cries eat away
the hearthstone.
Our empty, angry mouths
hunger for any words that cure.

IV

Nights while he's asleep
my mother kisses him.
"He can't fight me then. And alone
I can make love to him, to me."
Her eyes fill with warning:
"You'll get used to it, like I did."

At twelve my scout uniform
stained with forest seeds, above me
the crooning of white oak,
the crooning of a boy:
"Just one more time. One more time."

Until now.

V

One man and I
cautious as pilgrims
return together.

My father shoots up from the table,
away from my mother, quiet now, gray.
His forehead creases, eyes hammer,
turn back to the yams and greens
as if we violated their ground of
vegetables, children, dreams.

My words gather into knives
slicing the hunger: "I'm still your son."
As if the silent years between us
were reasons to forget, were reasons to forget.

SIGHTSEEING
for Richard

1.

Ocean City, Maryland:
a father and retarded son
shop the boardwalk
and amusement arcade.
Watching rides and pinball
machines the boy gyrates
limp, boneless hands
in furious circles,
trying to contain steel balls
and magical lights.

The father stops him,
holds him, but his body
keeps moving on its own
electricity.

2.

Manhattan IRT: bag ladies
in cut-off shoes, toes
swollen with gangrene
and black with soot,
bend newspapers and cloth
with great precision
into fold after fold after fold.

3.

D train crossing into Brooklyn
between Grand Street and Dekalb:
three men accost another for cigarettes,
then the gold bracelet, the gold watch.
In exchange for safe passage
commuters pretend blindness.

4.

Some sights catch your eyes
and never give them back.

Like the sun
curving into total eclipse.
No matter where you look
afterwards, you see
the cut of crescent
without the star.

GRANDMOTHER

1.
You say you don't remember
those years.
But what will they answer
when you run back
asking for more?

2.
Who are you?
The second son of your first son.
Who are you? See how my legs
open from the ground.
See the cutting birthmarks
on my wrists.
What did you say your name is?

3.
You say you can't recall
others like me: mute cousins
or your sons' bachelor sons
stuttering in padded cells
their names to metal windows.

4.
We need words for the hills that feed us.
We need bread from the grains you carry.

5.
This hour your breath tires easily.
Your arms fold like hurt wings.
You no longer remember the songs
that opened iron cages.

Your arms pock with all our ages.
Your burnt fingernails pull
at swollen knuckles, eyes go urgent
for wood frame, glass, and open air.

6.
Your silence

fills the space
between our homes
in Connecticut.

Your silence
sends me
South.

7.
From the Pee Dee River
upstream to log cabin pines
where my father was born

I call our names the same name
and listen for echoes that come.

KIN OF CROSSROADS

November drive through Fontainbleau,
past Napoleon's house and into Prieuré d'Avon
where the pines thin out and tufts
of mistletoe make nests in distant treetops.

We see the farmyard, the white house
fenced in, the wintering field
deserted of silent reaping.
"It was the Gurdjieff Institute,"
you point smiling.
"Jean Toomer was there back then."

And smiling you tell of your family poor
in *le Puy*, the Algerian War when you sided
with liberation fighters, the years in England
and Richard Wright whose briefcase
you now carry like skin.

In silence I wonder how many of us
came running fugitive
to drink this wine, seed this history,
(not of Napoleon, Versailles, or Orléans)

on ground we rake for kindling
and apples. We cut firewood, split black
walnuts and country cheese. Two reapers
of broken essentials, both hungry
for the red-burning moon.

for Michel Fabre,
les Bergeries

GETTING DIRECTIONS

If you are lucky enough to have lived in Paris as a young man, then, wherever you go for the rest of your life, it stays with you, for Paris is a moveable feast.

— *Hemingway*

Entering Paris
on a moveable feast of clouds
thick as an old man's beard,
I walk the streets kept clean
by the sweep of black
and Arab hands, their fists
tight on brooms of twigs.
One Senegalese face
studies mine.
His scarifications
of work and clan
point to the arc
of his bent arms,
to the dip
of his knees and ankles,
to feet far from ceremonial dance
when sewer water claimed him,
and to both of us
standing in the flow
leaving Paris.

RICHARD, RICHARD: AMERICAN FUEL

We both shuddered at the sound of Wright's burning body, quite audible in the still columbarium.

— *A witness.*

This far from Chicago and Natchez, Mississippi,
air is tight with the sound of difficult vowels
in *"adieu," "j'arrive,"* or *rue de la Liberté.*

November 8, 1960, away for thirteen years,
you speak at the American Church, musing
over changes since a journal entry in 1947:

"August 24: I have to remind myself
that I'm a Negro when I live in Paris.
There are whole days when I forget it.
France is, above all, a land of refuge."

Twenty days later as you lie in intensive care,
the ghost of a woman
visits the night nurse in Paris.

Whose last fingers test your brow for heat?
Whose girlish laughter ropes about your neck?

Then December. Cimetiére Pére Lachaise.
Friends gather with family. Smoke
squeals up from furnace to chimney.
Some shudder at the noisy mixture
of cremation and cold weather:

It is the chuckle
of Mary Dalton's sweet revenge,
the weighty echo of Bessie's moan.

RICHARD, RICHARD: AN AMERICAN HUNGER

We spread old manuscripts
like prayer cloth.
Some pages already parchment,
others in gray ink.
We feel where Bigger was born
between corrections,
how *Black Boy* was a true confession:
the American Hunger.

We search for your ear
to twelve million black voices
still listening here.
In attics we find your blues,
Big Boy's sweat,
and diamonds in Daniel's tracks
from underground.

And messages from Ellison,
Himes, and Baldwin
hanging on with teeth,
reading "beat that boy"
in transatlantic S.O.S.
calling richard, richard
to rue Monsieur le Prince,
rue de Lille, rue Jacob.

Richard, Richard
your voice has let us in.
Watch as Ellen takes us
to more tools. I touch
your thousand haikus
glued to cardboard like bricks.
We peel your pages one
by one to the skeleton
of travel. We hold
this exile which is meat,
these words of warning
offered as food.

for Michel Fabre and Ellen Wright
Paris, 1975

RICHMOND BARTHÉ: MEETING IN LYON

Lyon is a city of two rivers and Roman aqueducts
two thousand years old. I come by snake-roads
through the faces of three mountains, following
butterflies and the tracks of old bones.

I find you in the hour of molding and the time
of two rivers running here. Old fingers press
into clay. *The old ones touch the young
and help them to believe.*

I look into eyes that have seen through stone.
I listen to lips that gave language to the clay.
I touch the spidery hands that bent bronze into blues.

Africa Awakening, Meditation, Shoe Shine Boy,
Your blood hardens into stone. "Study nature,"
your say in riverwords that pulse two veins in Lyon
and leave Roman remains.

Your young-old eyes scorch the underbrush
in Mississippi, New York, Jamaica, Italy, and Sweden
as one flame. Bronze burning in black fingers
shed the thin skin, shed twisted muscles, shed
teeth and tears, leave the *inner music* and the
mountain butterflies to show the way.

2.

Two rivers swell in Lyon. Clean the old dust.
History is stone polished black.
Is blood and burnt bronze.

Your blood hardens into stone poems. *"What color is art?"*
"What color is love?" The questions and your crisp
eyes clean me, let me know the years you read muscles
torn from proud black chests, from open stilled mouths,
from wide nostrils and ebony bones and now reading me.

How I ache from being opened in these hours,
cut by these mountains, these rivers.

Who were you once in marble reincarnation? A statue?
A flesh carved god? A rock leading to mountaintops?
Who you will be next will meet me.
We cannot say goodbye here.

Rivers keep swelling and swelling, keep cutting out
mountains, keep washing the Roman stone.

One man lifts his wings. His neck veins stretch
alive. The sun boils him. This land heats
a kiln, this history a steady fire. Two rivers burn.

We heal ourselves
by our own believing.

The clay now bakes its own warning. The statued
marble collects the prize of blood. Can these words
too become breathing bronze, or rock cut tall
to ride horseback in Haiti, to swing machete
and still dance?

Lyon and St. Etienne,
France

CLIMBING MONTMARTRE

Take these thousand steps, these up-running shoes,
the orange/red/brownstone rooftops
studded like Arab faces in the sun. Take
my one African eye.

Take these white steps, these ladders up-growing
from the green, the marble-head dome with eyes
the flicking cameras of tourists, the franc rusted
fountains, the postcards, the translated prayers.

Take the beaded stained glass and the false
night naked inside, the nuns singing, the
statues looking cool, the candles leaning from light.

Langston in the twenties and old Locke too,
Cullen from the Hotel St. Pierre,
Wright from rue Monsieur le Prince, even too,
Martin came to climb Montmartre.

Take the fast breathing, the up-going,
the wide plane of rooftops frozen in a Paris mist.
the dignity of trodden stone descending to
subway sleepers, take my primitive feet
danced out and still.

Take the iron colored dust from *Gare du Nord,*
the pigeon feeders, the hundred smelling vendors,
the fast hands, the begging. Take jazz in
twisted TV antennas and wire clotheslines, or
my lips quivering, hands watching, holding.

Take this hill into the mind as you look
all over Europe; your clogged ears can't hear
the screaming, your pointed noses snuff out
blood and urine smells, your green eyes
don't see this body drop on angry gargoyles.

II
GOING TO AFRICA

When one is on the soil of one's ancestors, most anything can come to one . . .

— *Jean Toomer*

CHANGE OF TERRITORY

for D.M.

Shadow of the Pyrénées
on the train's steamy window
and the only clear spot
until snores from six sleepers
cloud it is the print
of my hand still waving
goodbye.

Revenir
means to come back, to return.
The *r* rolls up the tunnel of the throat
on a soft gargle. I count
the years we've traveled forth and back —
un, deux, trois, quatre, cinq
and now cease.

Alone
on this night train
to Madrid, I remember
our tongues and thighs
in irregular conjugation.
At customs I search for something
to declare. What is the Spanish word
for loss?

*La Puerta del Sol,
Paris-Madrid*

GOING TO AFRICA

"I am not the prodigal son," I said
to my mother who had come
to take me back. "I'm going to Africa,"

to see if my face colors her ground,
if my sadness thickens Sahara dust and famine,
if my wet season rains anything more than sweat.

I am not ashamed of searching.
But will she welcome me? I've left
English grammar, French phonetics, history,
anthropology notes, the King James Version.

And if not the color of her soil,
if my dance is toe-pointed and straight,
will she know me even as one lost son?
"I am not the prodigal," I said more softly.

And if I'm told, "You're American. Go home.
Africa doesn't want fugitives." Or turning
from my wheat skin, she awaits seeds deep
in famine soil and rainy human seasons,

I may find that a change of place
is nothing safe, and no other masks or moods
can tie back the cord that first fed me blues.

Paris

TOUR GUIDE: *La Maison des Esclaves*

He speaks of voyages:
men traveling spoon-fashion,
women dying in afterbirth,
babies clinging
to salt-dried nipples.
For what his old eyes still see
his lips have few words. Where
his flat thick feet still walk
his hands crack
into a hundred lifelines.

Here waves rush to shore
breaking news that we return
to empty rooms
where the sea is nothing calm.
And sun, tasting the skin
of black men,
leaves teeth marks.

The rooms are empty until he speaks.
His guttural French is a hawking trader.
His quick Wolof a restless warrior.
His slow, impeccable syllables
a gentleman trader. He tells
in their own language
what they have done.

Our touring maps and cameras ready
we stand in the weighing room
where chained men paraded firm backs,
their women open, full breasts,
and children,
rows of shiny teeth.

Others watched from the balcony,
set the price in guilders, francs,
pesetas and English pounds. Later,
when he has finished we too
can leave our coins
where stiff legs dragged
in endless bargain.

He shows how some sat knee-bent
in the first room.
Young virgins waited in the second.
In the third, already red,
the sick and dying
gathered near the exit to the sea.

In the weighing room again
he takes a chain to show us
how it's done. We take
photographs to remember,
others leave coins to forget.
No one speaks
except iron on stone
and the sea
where nothing's safe.

He smiles for he has spoken
of the ancestors: his, ours.
We leave quietly, each alone,
knowing that they who come after us
and breaking
in these tides will find
red empty rooms
to measure long journeys.

Ile de Gorée, Senegal

SANDAGA MARKET WOMEN

We take the weight of children in the sun,
their heads bobbing from our backs
their mouths opening in quick sleep
with food for flies at market noon.

We take the weight of baskets and clay pots
fat with mangoes, printed cloth, and bread.
The heat that called us here now burns
the road leading home from market talk

that takes the weight of indigo and ochre weaves,
sales of anklets hammered out of dollars,
French francs, or studded with cowries
and African gold on ebony skin.

We take the weight of languages and signs,
commercial English, Dutch, and Portuguese.
Words beating from stretched black skin
rhyme in Wolof for our songs and dancing

to take the weight of children lost
to oceans in the North and West. They
who once sailed into centuries, who now
return in lipstick and with greenback hands.

Dakar, Senegal

VOODOO MAMBO: TO THE TOURISTS

Sifting flour onto the ground
I draw their signs from memory.
It's been done before. You want
to recognize my prayer: *Gods,*
loa, ancestral guests
we salute you. First with water,
then rum, then fire.

Listen well. Those sounds
crowding the night are gods
crossing the seas, reaching me.
Watch those shadows lift into music.
You want me to dance as easily
or sing? Do not expect me to smile.
I am not who you think I am.

Do you think you can pay to know
what I know? The soul travels quickly
from a body touched by drums.
Shadows burn and the breath
stands still outside. And outside myself
I see myself dancing, the dove limp
in my grip until its head
drops free.

I circle, and I circle again
through blood and rum and limbs
no longer mine, nor this voice
of steel and drums crying:
*my body drinks like empty
riverbeds I remember crossing.*

Maybe I am Erzilie, that man
Ogoun-Feraille, and others Agwé,
Baron Samedi, Damballah, Legba.
Our dozen feet rake back into the soil
what could have come alive
had we really given up ourselves
to pigeon blood, or wood coals on flesh.

For you we call out any names
but the real ones. Perhaps.
This is how the gods become us.

*for Catuxo Badillo,
Port-au-Prince, Haiti*

ZORA NEALE HURSTON:
"I'LL SEE YOU WHEN
YOUR TROUBLE GETS LIKE MINE"

for Robert Hemenway, Alice Walker, Sherley Williams

> — "She didn't come to you empty."
> *C. E. Bolen at Hurston's funeral.*

I cross over from the other shore,
sit among you on the rock of song:
Gambling Song, Geechee Song, Wake-up Chant
from the sawmill camp, Railroad Lining Song:

Line down that bar — Hah —
Line down that bar!

Shove it over, Hey, Hey!
O can't you line it
Shaka-laka-laka-laka-laka-laka — Huh!
O can't you try.

I conjure voice out of hammer and rail,
take hold of steel without warning.
Until you have lived it,
I make of every hour
a moment you thought you knew.

I got a rainbow
wrapped and tied around my shoulder.
I got a rainbow wrapped and tied.

When Lomax asked me how, I told him
I just get in with the people.
If they sing I take part
until I learn all the verses.
Then, when it is in my memory,
I take it with me wherever I go.

Now you, children, line by line,
can take it from there.

HARLEM FOOTAGE

(Pathé Films, c. 1929)

Back then in Harlem
we couldn't go
to the Cotton Club:
Reserved For Whites Only.
So we strutted our stuff
at the Renaissance Ballroom
and at Smalls' Paradise.
Now in a silent newsreel
we see what we couldn't
see before: black women
in a chorus line, all
headrags, aprons,
housecoats and broken shoes,
scrub pails and mops
in a slow drag downstage,
mouths moving in a song
we cannot hear. Maybe
a downhome spiritual:
*Nobody knows the trouble
I've seen,* or a work-song
in 4/4 dance beat:
*I ain't no ways tired,
ain't no ways tired, Lord.*
On cue from the big band
mops and pails give way to
stagelights from wide eyes

and grinning teeth. Then out
from under such uniforms
of service come ostrich feathers,
sequined leotards and caps,
tap shoes with fringed anklets
marking rhythm and sway.
White patrons just as quick
tap their coins and drinks
to the syncopated shuffle
hidden all this time by those
they had always suspected
were really just out
to have a good time.

ANGELS OF ASCENT

to Robert Hayden

You know us, all of us, by the tracks
we left in Norfolk and Nashville,
Ann Arbor and Detroit. You know us
by the hollow of our screams
shuttling from street to street:
cautious Stefan, zany me, and Richard
with his chattering teeth on edge.

One of us stayed with you for a time
in Tennessee, someone you claimed
as "orphan boy" and hugged
late at night. Your words
conjuring mysteries of the body
sent him looking for kin.

And still we search. You hear us
hissing like the sea at shipboards,
whisking our arms in first flight.
Your name fluttering in our talk:
"Robert Hayden gone a-movering,
movering home."

Once in New Haven I shook your hand,
held onto that flesh of words. You knew
what mystery children we are, how we ache
in dark and dreamy valleys of paradise
for absolute gravity, with no names
for the spaces we inhabit, nor any
last tears for being there.

III
BOBO BAOULÉ

BOBO BAOULÉ

I

Take me to the water
(After a legend as told by Bernard Dadié)

Fleeing into night and day and night again and
troubling the forest with our fears of capture,
hiding from brushfire and a rain of spears
that tell us our villages are sacked,
we arrive without fetish or food at the edge
of a dangerous, dangerous shore, all of us
anxious for the message of the waves:

"Give up, give up your most treasured
possession. Give up, give up
what you value most high."

And we keep coming to the water
No way to cross over
We keep coming to the water
No way to turn back.

Clanging bracelets, armbands of cowries,
then anklets in leather and beads, silver
rings and bright woven cloth, all this
piles high and higher but not high enough
to calm the raging surf:

"Give up, give up what you value
most high. Give up, give up
best of black skin and blood."

Anger. Murmurs of dissent and disbelief.
A laying on of hands. And you, Queen Pokou,
mother, lift me with nervous fingers.
Your face hollows like a talking drum losing
voice. Your eyes sink like weights for gold.
You step forward from the crowd and toss
me trembling into rapids that are troubling,
troubling, troubling with death.

And they keep coming to the water
For a way to cross over
They keep coming to the water
For a way to go on.

I cannot rise for air. Many must think
me dead as I do too with some scaly
darkness coming over, over me. A great
fish has swallowed me whole, giving breath
and rounded eyes to see hippopotamuses
lined in a row and on their backs my people
crossing into safety. Their thankful
praying quiets the surf and last I hear
is the voice of my mother drumming pain:
"Baoulé, he is gone. Baoulé, he is dead."

"No, no," I try to say. "No, I'm still alive!"
But the Great Fish swims the opposite way.
"Do not be afraid," the Great Fish tells me.
"Do not be afraid. You have given them a name."

Coming to the water they
Found a way over
Coming to the water they
Found a new home.

II

O wasn't that a wide river?
Got one more river to cross.

For years it seems we travel like this:
Myself alone inside the greater skin.
Silvery and dark is my growing there,
stretching arms and legs to the dance
of waves. I eat what the Great Fish eats.
From his round eyes I see how dark
this water is, how dangerous, how deep,
as dreams of walking on land fill my sleep.

Then on a leap we break the surface,
the Great Fish and I. We see enormous
woods and sails speeding across the sea.
Down below again I think I hear some black
man's cry and a splash and splash some more.
The body wrapped in chains, fighting for release.

"Do not be afraid," the Great Fish tells me.
"Do not be afraid. They have changed their names."

Sudden cough and blood like he is hooked,
and fighting metal, he vomits me. I awake
upon a white beach shore, clutching around
at this, the answer to my prayer for ground:

III

"You there, *nigra*."

"Baoulé."

"Huh?"

"Baoulé."

"Naw, boy. You Bobo, now."

"Baoulé."

"Bawlay? You mean Bobo Bawlay."

"Baoulé. Ba-ou-lé."

Whips snake on my skin. The bite
of leather fangs. My back
a track of teeth. At my head
guns ready to smoke:

"You there, Bobo."

"Bobo."

"Nice boy, Bobo."

On the edge of my breath: *Baoulé.*
And laboring for centuries on dry rock
moving, moving, moving toward the sea,
hungry for salt and the taste of scales

I keep coming to the water
For a way to cross over
I keep coming to the water
For a way to go home.

Martinique, Cuba, Haitian sun.
New Orleans market and Virginia Beach.
Little Rock. Selma. Birmingham.
East St. Louis. Chicago. Harlem, New York.

"I am afraid," I call out everywhere.
"I am afraid that we have lost our names."

Then the voice of the Great Fish answers:
"No more troubling, troubling the water.
You got to trouble, trouble the land."

And he is gone from my aching ears forever.

IV

Dear Mom,

Arrived safely! Hope everything is fine back home. Crossing
the Atlantic took longer than expected. We had a day's stop-
over in Paris and I saw the Eiffel Tower. It was grand! I
arrived in Abidjan on an Air Afrique DC-10 and found the
city full of supermarkets, discos, taxi cabs, and even an
indoor ice skating rink nearby.

Last week I started my Peace Corps project in an upcountry
village among the Baoulé people. Ever hear of them? They're
real friendly and make you feel quite at home. I'm learning
their language by practicing a song they sing about Queen
Pokou, who sacrificed her son to an angry river god. I'll sing
it for you when you visit next spring.

Give my regards to all the Bawlays. Especially Great-Uncle
Bobo and Cousin Jim. That was a swell *bon voyage* party
you all threw for me. You'll like the Ivory Coast, I'm sure.
It's full of surprises.

Write soon,
Bobby

IV

HEMISPHERES

FINGERING THE JAGGED GRAINS

The blues is an impulse to keep the painful details and episodes of a brutal experience alive in one's aching consciousness, to finger its jagged grain, and to transcend it . . .

— *Ellison*

1.

Blue notes from Baltimore and Charlotte, N.C.
Albert Murray riffing on Bearden's
long vamp to his own fast train,
a whistling northbound steel-smoking hound,
and the tracks of writing tell it true:
"There were no bad trains, but everybody
used to think of passenger trains
as good trains."

Well, right in the gallery
we almost had church!

This time in Brooklyn, before the first killing
frost or the frozen steel of subways and tenement
pipes, Teddy Wilson and son heat up on piano
and bass, fingering Ellington's A train
back through Catfish Row. Upstairs the melody
is Bearden playing Bearden: *Out Chorus, Tenor Spot,*
Stomping at the Savoy and *Carolina Shout,*
calling up J. P. Johnson and baptism in the Pee Dee.
Scooter conducts the orchestra,
Maudell Sleet takes a bow.
And Rinehart solos up from underground.

It is the elegance of ritual: Bearden, Ellison
and Murray cutting the jagged grains: patchwork
figures in silhouette, blue notes in calico
and quilting under glass. *What did I do*
to be so black and blue? Electric blue, fire
and fuchsia in the sky. Lightning, lonesome blue.
Cut out legs, fingers and bebop eyes
shape the uncreated features of face and race.
Found objects of the territory:
Mecklenberg County to Harlem and back.
Cloth and color in piano stride.

What did I do? You lived, you lived!
And the jagged grains *so black and blue*
open like lips about to sing.

2.

Everywhere women: Miss Sheba and Queen Susannah.
High butt women. Thick thigh women.
Luvernia or sweet Liza in the grass.
Maudell Sleet riffing Mary Rambo
don't you weep, don't you weep.
Faces cut from Benin masks with jaws
carved out of hunger and loss and joy.
Women in gardens, bathing from washtubs,
of just making love with those great huge hands.
Pieces of fried-chicken-tablecloths
and bedspreads waiting a long good night
of Carolina quilting and African weaves
and those wide and wrinkled hands
fingering the empty spaces.

Black Nativity:
High Cotton, Mother & Child.
Eyes like liquid marbles
in a blaze of sun.

Afro-American Gothic:
Miss Bertha & Mr. Seth.
25 X 18. Collage on board.
From a private collection.

"The last time I saw Liza," Bearden's
handwriting said, "was down at the station
when I left for Pittsburgh on the 5:13."
The Daybreak Express. The heartbreak stride
to Harlem where Rinehart played the keys.

54

3.

Rinehart, Rinehart, where you been?
Round the corner and back again.
Boomerang!
Jagged grains.
Boomerang!
Jagged masks:

Faceless picaro cool-strutting through collage,
you smoked glasses and high-water threads,
fedora hat and patent leather dogs, you midnight
indigo of mood and magic, act cut from sack-cloth
shadow: Ellison playing Bearden playing Ellison.

Rinehart, you fooled them all
and you sure fooled me. I know all about
the Pee Dee and Carolina yams, but not
that the grains could talk that talk:

"Do Jesus!"
And he did.

Yeah, Rine, we know where you been.
But baby, where you going?

4.

South. To a new old place. Back
to the track and the clickety-clack
like someone's Saturday child.

Cool Scooter, you so Louisiana sweet.
Fast-tracking Scooter, you real southern sweet.
Your daddy is Rinehart, your mama Maudell Sleet.

"When I was old enough," the handwriting said,
"I found out what Liza's mother did for a living."

And it was blue. Steel-cutting blue.
Luzanna Cholly riffing Mr. Seth,
and Murray playing Ellison playing Bearden
playing Murray on infinite multiples of three:

Tri-angular. A three-note chord.
Triptych and three part harmony.
Alto. Tenor. Bass.

Ellison on Painting:
"The problem for the plastic artist
is not one of telling but of *revealing*."

Bearden on Fiction:
Pepper Jelly Lady (1981)
"The trains in the stories she told
always ran North.
I used to look at the sky
and think of storybook dragons."

Murray on Music and More:
Stomp, stomp, stomping the blues.
"Young men who become the heroes
do so by confronting and slaying dragons.
Improvisation is the ultimate skill."

And at the Brooklyn Museum
Teddy Wilson on piano.

5.

Those hands cut from paper bag groceries and grace,
those hands opening like lips on a blues,
finger the jagged grains of a long, long, long
remembered time. Can you see it? Can you hear it?
What did I do to be so black and blue?
Rinehart, Scooter and Maudell Sleet:
Character, Consciousness and Collage.

New York, 1981-82

HEMISPHERES

I

He come out the backwater towns
and a log cabin overrun with creepers.
He come off the road by the river Pee Dee
cutting North Carolina way down into South.
He come out the gullies and rusted
yard pump, water chilling to the bone.

He'd draw bucketfuls for his Mama
so she'd have something to cook and clean with.
He come out the South, farming,
and she watched him leave, her first boy,
cutting tracks to Connecticut out of Pee Dee,
a name more easy to forget than to remember.

And when his Mama came North
out of old age and sickness,
then went back in a coffin, he told me,
"Don't come to the funeral.
You probably glad she dead."

I used to sing about dreamers, beautiful
dreamers. And when he pushed me to the other
side of the bed once he was through, once
he saw it was me he was having, not some
woman in his head, he said, "Why don't you
stop that singing. Just shut up."
So I sang to myself from then on.

"And don't bother fixing my breakfast no more.
You got nails in your voice, woman. Nails."
He knew all about nails. He was a handyman.
He built things.

And it really was me he was having.
Not anybody else. You kids is proof.

Me? I come out Irmo, you know.
Just beyond Columbia, South Carolina.
I learned to drive a jalopy cause my Daddy,
whose name was Pink and who was black
as pitch, black as a country night full of
chaingang runaways, had to get to church.

I come out the woods back of the house
Pink built himself, where he buried
my Mama. You want to see
her grave? What you scared of?
I come out that grave. You do too.

So I figured out myself how the gears
and accelerator worked quick enough
to get us both to praying ground.
I didn't come North till later on.
Then I really was in orbit.
All up around him, your Daddy.

But he started pushing me to my side the bed
and wouldn't let me touch him.
And when I did touch him, he never knew it
cause he was sleep by then.
I sure wasn't gonna leave him.
If he wanted to leave me, he could.
He did.

What am I going to do? Can't go South.
Ain't nothing there for me except woods
and two graves now. Don't think
I'm mad about it. Shit.
Where are you kids now I need you?
Where are you, boy?

II

Travelin'

Between North and South and a language
of gutturals and sweet "aah's,"
between thighs breaking open quick as a train
pulling into Brooklyn from the Bronx.

Across steel and the conversations
of shoppers going home, the pain mounts
in a conspiracy of limbs, and I can't walk.
Legs ache, stomach cramps up, and you
just ride, ride, ride between my tracks,
between metal and skin, right at the "o"
of the body between you and me.

Mint tea in Marrakech in a storm of sun:
I should have asked his name, followed him
out of the market and maze of wares
stacked high. The guidebook says,
This is the tomb of the Kings. This, the Mosque.
O sinner man, where can I run to?

Bamako, Dakar, Abidjan, Lagos, Ife, Ibadan.

Crossing the Sahara by Boeing jet,
everywhere the red-orange glow of sandstorm.
This could be Irmo or Pee Dee.
The sun descending. Heat standing still.
Yards upon yards of indigo cotton
screen out the sun and guard
the closed borders below:

Bamako, Dakar, Abidjan, Lagos, Ife, Ibadan.

. . .

Gemini.
Gregarious of May and June.
I divide in half
at the body's
equator.
My hemispheres
lift into orbit.

Where are you
now that I need you?

. . .

And reaching into the sky
from African soil, I thought about death
at the scrape of metal wings
traveling, traveling.
"The hardest thing about it,"
a Maasai elder once said,
"is leaving the ground."

Itinerant weaver in Grand Bassam,
left Ghana in the uncertainty of cowries
to shuttle warp and weft in a gloom
of thread, plied into kente cloth
from twigs at his toes. Fingers gnarled
from pulling, pulling, pulling for a price,
anxious for English and broad smiles.
"For family back home," I said.

Where are you now that I need you?

"Travelin'."

. . .

Beware all round shapes:
earth, moon, sun,
kneecaps, elbows, eyeballs,
and the ridge of any man or woman
that can pull you in deep.
Beware globes of the body
moving on an axis
of easy pleasure.

"I can take you around the world,
to the end of the world," he smiled.

"Travelin'," I said.

Where are you, now that I need you,
now that I need you, now that I need you?

III

Coming Home

Dried flowers like eyes in shock.
Two trees cut down, grass wild
between the separate stumps.
The house all asleep.

I come out the Pee Dee and the Nile
in Connecticut. She looks up and asks me,
"You gonna spend the night?
When you leaving?"

I hunt through grade school papers,
newspaper photos of me in a Boy Scout
uniform grinning yellow and cracked
like the skin between my toes

or the spots on my face. I look
into the mirror and remember
wearing her dresses. I'd flex
my arms like a moth at a light
and hang my painted nails as flags.

My mother hides her grey Afro
under a ten-dollar wig,
her brownskin eyes about to knit
the family back. She says,

"I'm so unhappy. I'm so unhappy,"
and the tracks on her face
cut the long way home.

I can't answer for the years
away or how I've grown.
My face draws tight, cheeks
folding in like the corners
of an aging photograph.

"How long this time," she asks,
"how long you staying?"